Believing in Two Bodies

Believing in Two Bodies

Poems by

Gilbert Allen

Cover design by Shay Culligan

ISBN: 978-1-952326-67-7

Kelsay Books
502 South 1040 East, A-119
American Fork, Utah, 84003

In Memory of James McConkey

and Gladys/Jean

Acknowledgments

The author wishes to thank the editors of the publications in which the following poems first appeared, sometimes in slightly different form:

Able Muse: "Nostradamus in Hempstead," "Flesh"
The American Scholar: "A Wedding Wish"
The Cortland Review: "Plenty"
Crazyhorse: "But to Begin It"
Delmarva Review: "Right to Work"
The Georgia Review: "Bees in Lavender"
Illuminations: "Lost and Found"
Measure: "Uncles," "This Branching Room," "Forty Years North of Dreamland"
Miramar: "Dead Man's Curve"
The New Verse News: "Make America Great Back Then," "My Mother Teaches Me to Type"
The Pedestal Magazine: "Good Luck"
Pembroke Magazine: "Symbolic Gestures"
Sewanee Theological Review: "Looking Out the Window of a Virgin Fast-Food Restaurant," "Sixty Winters"
Southern Poetry Review: "Reckoning"
The Southern Review: "The Assistant," "Timber," "The World of Tomorrow," "The Clarinet," "Two Become One Flesh"
Valparaiso Poetry Review: "Primary Research," "Blueberries"
Your Daily Poem: "In the Natural History Museum"
Zone 3: "Making Tea for the Millennium"

The documentary film *The World of Tomorrow* (narrated by Jason Robards, produced and directed by Tom Johnson and Lance Bird, 1981) helped the author to imagine the world of his young parents: Marie Dawn Skocik and Joseph Aloysius Allen.

"Two Become One Flesh" was featured on *Poetry Daily* on August 17, 2016.

"The Assistant" received the Robert Penn Warren Prize from *The Southern Review*.

"My Mother Teaches Me to Type" received a Porter Fleming Award from the Greater Augusta Arts Council.

"But to Begin It," "A Wedding Wish," and "Bees in Lavender" were reprinted in *A Millennial Sampler of South Carolina Poetry*.

"Primary Research" and "Dead Man's Curve" were reprinted in *Archive: South Carolina Poetry Since 2005*.

"Forty Years North of Dreamland" was reprinted in *South Carolina Voices: Poetry and Prose*.

"The Assistant," "Flesh," "Timber, "Making Tea for the Millennium," "But to Begin It," "Symbolic Gestures," "Bees in Lavender," and "Good Luck" appeared in the chapbook *Body Parts*.

Special thanks to Bill Aarnes for his suggestions in revising "The Assistant" and to Bill Rogers for his advice in revising "The First Days."

Contents

I. Nostradamus in Hempstead

Primary Research   15
Nostradamus in Hempstead   17
Plenty   18
Looking Out the Window of a Virgin Fast-Food
    Restaurant   20
Make America Great Back Then   21

II. The Assistant

The Assistant   25

III. Flesh

Flesh   33
Lost and Found   34
Timber   37
Making Tea for the Millennium   38
Right to Work   40

IV. The World of Tomorrow

The World of Tomorrow   43

V. But to Begin It

The Clarinet   55
Uncles   57
This Branching Room   58
Reckoning   60
But to Begin It   61

VI. The First Days

The First Days   65

VII. Dead Man's Curve

A Wedding Wish   79
Two Become One Flesh   80
Blueberries   81
Dead Man's Curve   82
Symbolic Gestures   84

VIII. Forty Years North of Dreamland

Forty Years North of Dreamland   89

IX. My Mother Teaches Me to Type

Sixty Winters   101
Bees in Lavender   103
My Mother Teaches Me to Type   105
In the Natural History Museum   106
Good Luck   107

The body dies; the body's beauty lives.
                    —Wallace Stevens

I. Nostradamus in Hempstead

Primary Research

for Lynne Shackelford

Scrolling through microfilm in the library,
scavenging facts as yet undigitized,
trying to fathom what's become my home—
Greenville, South Carolina—I've been lost
all afternoon in 1941,
that summer of DiMaggio and Williams.

The big barn dance at Textile Hall; twenty-
eight Confederate veterans still alive;
the first dual-lane paved highway in the state
to be completed by the next July.
Forty stills smashed by the county sheriffs;
the first-ever first-aid class for Negroes
sponsored by the local (white) Red Cross.

A peacetime blackout of all service stations;
fifteen-cent movies, peaches fifty cents
a bushel; and a photo of an eight-
year-old Dick Riley, bravely modeling
a back-to-school "teal gabardine wash suit"
for Belk-Simpson's downtown department store.
Cole Brothers' Circus, featuring Jack Dempsey
(with elephants!) performing at the Fair Grounds
on Labor Day weekend.

                    And then I see
an AP story from Hempstead, New York—
my first home town, beginning ten years later.
A P-39 Army pursuit plane
flown by Lieutenant Roy W. Scott

tore through electric lines, then ruptured a water
main when it exploded—on a quiet street
where two preschoolers (one boy and one girl)
played in the grass. Both sets of parents burned
their hands and arms, trying to pull away
the gasoline-soaked clothes from writhing bodies.

Both children died in Meadowbrook Hospital:
Casper, the young son of the Cucios;
Georgene, the four-year-old daughter of Dr.
and Mrs. Arthur Kramer.

              And I remember
not just that name, his office, but his visiting
me at 89 Florence Avenue,
bedridden—when I had measles or chicken pox,
his practiced hand upon my blazing forehead,
his saying I was a very lucky boy,
his saying I'd be all right soon—then closing
up his big black bag and leaving, whistling,
while my own mother whispered *that poor man*
(so only I could hear) but nothing else.

Nostradamus in Hempstead

When *Look* published that cover photograph
I still can see—white asparagus sprouting
from an open gantry, and the letters
THE SOARING SIXTIES stenciled above the stalk—
how could I not envision every era
of my new future? I alliterated
all them out—

        The Swinging Seventies;
The Eating Eighties; and the Naughty Nineties—
shadowing, with nothing but my language
as my lantern, *Saturday Night Fever;*
Greed Is Good; and Monica Lewinsky.

Yet I stopped before I got to where
I am now—probably because I couldn't
imagine this age, older than my already
old father was in 1959.
So this millennium's decade has remained
a mystery, an opera in which all
blood must be music in its own sweet time.
Let's call it history. The Haughty Aughts—
where nothing could surprise us anymore
except to see Black Muslims on our money.
God's on our side. The Bible's not in French.
Even the Amish are wearing Nikes now.

Plenty

Porgy and Bess, Third-Grade Chorus, 1959

They put on their headrags
at home, humming till burnt cork
(left over from Halloween) spread
from their mothers' long fingers, surrounded
their lips. Then it was safe
once again to open their mouths
and sing *I got plenty* . . .
No mule! Twenty
Mule Team Borax! Misery?
A word wagging its tail, under the dinner table,
where they'd fed it whatever
they never wanted.

No rug on *this* floor!
Wall-to-wall carpet.
And more bagels than locks
in their neighborhood, that's
the way to be, kids drifting
into one another's houses
at the first scent
Saturday mornings.

No cars of their own, not yet.
That evening, they sat in back
and rode the train of Good
& Plenty, these eight-year-old commuters,
without newspapers, shaking the candy box—
until the school they'd never seen
glowing was born again through the windshield,

a new galaxy with a parking lot.
And, as they left those hubcapped
finned rockets, as they dropped
from their parents' hands to run

for the risers waiting inside,
they didn't have to look up, they were
the stars in the Long Island sky, all prized,
all free.

Looking Out the Window of a Virgin Fast-Food Restaurant

Greenville, South Carolina, 2000

Would Jefferson have slit his throat?
New asphalt, plastic pennants, and
the only yeoman farmer here
is waving a Confederate
flag from a pickup bed—free hand
ready to baptize a passing queer
with an empty Budweiser.

Chewing my last French fry, I gaze
across Highway 291.
Everything unnecessary,
new, and gleaming in this day's
descending—Eckerd, Sav-A-Ton
Gas, All We Have Must Go. My
supersized sweet tea.

Behind, a man pleads with his daughter.
*For God's sake, honey, please, don't
mess yourself up.* A full cup splats
the floor, splashes my pants. *Water,
just water,* he reassures, *it won't
stain.* To go with his *don't worrys*
she giggles out some *sorrys*—

sings them, this woman-in-waiting,
who'll be waiting for a sunset
spread on a 2020 floor,
who'll scuttle it simply in creating
a world simple as the one she wet—
a lost America, adored
bright spill, remembered chord.

Make America Great Back Then

*The first African slaves were brought to the North
American colony of Jamestown, Virginia, in 1619.*
　　　　　　　　　　　　　　　　　—History.com

Four hundred years ago, we needed you.
Turn Air Force One into a time machine.
Bless colonists with your enlightened views.
Four hundred years ago, we needed you
to end this chain migration's witches' brew
before it started. Be our go-between!
Four hundred years ago, we needed you.
Turn Air Force One into a time machine.

II. The Assistant

The Assistant

[Anna Coleman] Ladd's most unusual contribution was made during World War I. In 1917 she accompanied her husband to France where both of them served in the American Red Cross (ARC). He ran a hospital and she opened a studio known as ARC Portrait Studio where she made "new faces" for disfigured soldiers. . . . In some cases, because plastic surgery was not advanced enough at the time, these masks served as a permanent cosmetic device. In total she made over 60 masks and trained others to continue her work.

—Karen Tenney-Loring

I. *ATTENTION! ARTISTES AMÉRICAINES!*

How could I resist?
Must be able
to deal with extreme unpleasantness.
Fine. I'd loved
The Armory Show. I was sick
of the sycophants who still dragged their easels
out into the Connecticut countryside
each morning—cows
at grass, painting
cows at grass.
A child behind a camera
could do as well!
I'd come to Paris to slash
my canvases with red and black,
to make war come alive.

**

II. The Interview

Mrs. Ladd never stops
smiling. She wears
her hair, a halo
with pins, primly. She unrolls

25

my newest painting, nods,
and asks if I can draw.

"I see I have insulted you,
my dear. That's good."

She leans across the table,
hands me a photograph
(generic man in uniform),
then paper, colored chalk.

"Imagine flesh tones, please.
I'll be back in half an hour."

I almost leave.
I don't.

**

III. Val-de-Grâce Military Hospital

Anna makes the castings, and I paint.
Sometimes, it's like collage—adding glass eyes,
silver-sliver eyebrows and mustaches.
The hopeless are the easiest for us,
the easiest to satisfy. A circus
in reverse! For which a full-face mask
of normalcy—which had been blasted off—
hides shell craters the war made permanent.
There's nothing to match up, to camouflage.
Just strap it on, and send them on their way.
The ones with tongues thank us. The ones without?
They shake our hands, and leave by the same door.

The partials are more challenging—to fuse
the artificial with the salvageable
real—to blend the lines and colors into
one whole. Whole! The horror of that word
and what it holds within! Holes of noses,
chins, ears, mandibles we cover with
crafted copper. The Tin Noses Shop.
That's what they call the London institute.
We've named ours The Portrait Studio,
a dignified attempt at dignity.

**

IV. *Après Le Bon Voyage*

Anna's bound for Massachusetts.
Before she left, she trained
two sculptors (French) to make the casts
to cover what constrained

the doctors to concede defeat.
"Our work begins where that
of surgeons ends." Her husband ran
the hospital, fears art

for her will never be the same
again. *Triton Babies,*
Anna's old embodiment of
"the joy of youth and dreams,"

awaits her: the bronze warden
of Boston Public Garden.

**

V. Preliminary Studies Continue

I meet with each man, privately,
inquire what he wants to see

in his new face. Day after day,
my old portfolio walks away.

Some of them want "the same"—others
want a difference, better or worse.

One demanded a "dashing" scar
on his new cheek—for "ocular

distraction," as he deftly said,
before inviting me to bed.

I smiled, "I'm tempted"—his reward—
then tightened his elastic cord.

**

VI. Results Satisfactory: Patient Discharged

Most want to take a walk,
wait in the railway station,
loiter on the sidewalk.
Most want to take a walk
with no averted stares, hushed talk—
just idle conversation.
Most want to take a walk,
wait in the railway station.

**

VII. Her Last Day

My final favorite, the one
with no eyes, tells me
he *hears* the difference
on the train to Val-de-Grâce.
No gasps, no cries
from children anymore! He leaves.

I make myself a mask
true to his maskless face. I strap it on.
I'm one of my old paintings, red and black,
strolling, on this splendid day, in search
of cows and grass. Watch
them all stare, in silence—at
the ruined art no man
could ruin, not even in the dark.

**

III. Flesh

Flesh

I'm painting the new master bedroom with
a color I can't quite identify.
It looked great on the sample sheet. Peach? Pink?
Beige? All three?

Nordic Mist, the can insists. Until I
remember the color—from the Crayola box
of my almost-middle-class childhood. *Flesh.*
And how it matched

my skin, if not quite perfectly, well then
well enough to escape my notice. And I
now wonder, as I never had before,
about my

classmates who stared at that dull stick of color,
and at that name, and drew upon themselves,
to behold not camouflage but something
different. Worse

or better? And who had the big box at home?
For them, *Flesh* would've been concealed in others'
mittens. Even if they'd ripped it off, it would've
remained pointless

and perfect—something for their little brother
to put into his mouth, on their command,
and crush between his teeth. Never becoming
funny or grand

as they'd imagined, just a goddamn mess
they could've melted on the radiator
in the schoolhouse that'd already taught them
to know better.

Lost and Found

I hadn't been playing.
Just sauntering
along, a sunny afternoon,
a shortcut to
somewhere—despite
my motion, what newspapers
proclaim an innocent
bystander. But the only

one who'd fit.

So they lowered
me through
the frame
of the awning
window
of the basement
of the ruined
schoolhouse

and let go.

My feet struck the earth
six feet below the earth
they'd come from.
The air hovered, so full
of dust and light
that dust and light
seemed the same.
So I could see—

inside a bookcase

lying like a forefather
lost in his longest nap—
the foul ball, horsehide
unraveled, dark
as a spoiled apple
hardly worth saving.
And after I'd pitched
it up, they thanked me,

laughed, and left.

The next year the suburbs
would reach out with their long
manicured fingers. The whitewashed
rubble would be razed
and resurrected, miraculous
as new money. But this
wasn't next year.
This was hours

and hours

among the bindings
of damp books I couldn't
read, among desks with dry
inkwells, and those cracked
blackboards so small even *my* hands
could hold them—all stained
with stale incense
only half chalk.

These walls weren't going anywhere.

As I longed through their glass
teeth at the lowering
sun, I knew I'd be here
forever, in that new, old dark,
so frightened I wasn't even
frightened—just lost
within the false certainty
of silence.

So, like a perfect student,

I sat at the nearest desk
and slept. I don't remember
who got me out, or when,
or why, although
it must have happened.
I never asked, and now
there is no one
to ask—only a beautiful house

no decent man or woman

can afford. But I'd like
to think my saviors
and my imprisoners
the same—lost
as the child put there
sixty years ago, lost
as that other child
more or less

brought back.

Timber

My body lies over the ocean
O bring back my body to me
we boys used to shout
in music class, over
that pleading piano and Miss
Bonnie Armbruster's grand, maternal sighs.
Next September, when music became

an elective we didn't
elect, we forgot our unknowing
emendation, though we sang along
with the transistor to dozens
of tunes with identical backbeats, badly,
like carpenters building their first wall, voices
cracked full of raw daylight.

Beaten back, aching all over creation,
I've more than begun
the slow voyage away from
that shore—still within shouting
distance, maybe, but diminishing toward
the leveled horizon. And I remember
and long for the body

that always was deaf as a timber
but could fake it for
a while—as it came to us
unasked, unnoticed, as air, as
it briefly lingered
as the sea shivers
it, piece by piece.

Making Tea for the Millennium

End, the microwave shouts
at me, *End   End   End.*
I'll let it steep.
It's a day for endings,
Earl Grey, all on the same bleary
insistent note that speaks for itself
again, like a smoke alarm
with a battery almost, but not
quite, dead.

Once I stood at a funeral
with fake flowers so real, sensible
ladies sneezed at them, sniffling
as they leaned over
he looks so natural
their mascara smearing
with tears till their faces

were Frank Umeena's penitent
composition, after Mr. LaConniss
demonstrated for the class
"the one problem with charcoal"
with his spreading left hand, then
told Frank he wasn't finished,
no, he hadn't gotten to the end
just yet, and handed him
a Number Two pencil, a new
sheet of bond.

And he was right, we were
only ten, it was 1961, even
the dropouts, even the volunteers
had seven more years
at least, except

for Ronnie, who stopped
his stolen Firebird with a telephone pole
Just, he managed to tell
the towering police, *to see
how it sounded, up close
in my face, how it tasted.*

Right to Work

The Volvo decision to join BMW and Mercedes in South Carolina spotlights the success of Southern states in attracting . . . non-union plants.
—James R. Healey, USA Today

I don't remember where I'd heard
the phrase. But that summer
when Mom said I was old enough,
led me to the mower,

pulled the cord to get me started,
I stalled and grinned. "At least
I have the right to work!" At that
she shoved me sideways, faced

the weeping willow tree, engaged
the clutch, and didn't stop
for a full hour—while I watched
like a Pinkerton cop

her perfect union lines
parade across our lawn.

IV. The World of Tomorrow

The World of Tomorrow

*for my mother's words
and for my father's silences*

1961

Ten years old, old enough
to think myself
of some use, I strut
into the garage, to wheel out our first
gas-powered lawnmower, my mother
watching, warning *Don't scratch
the car.* I'm careful

but I take my eyes off the teal
Oldsmobile 98. Stop
for a tarnished ashtray on a makeshift
shelf, sigodlin, nailed between two studs
of the unfinished wall.

It would never be finished.

I hold it in both
hands, one cupping
the ash-blackened crater next to
the copper ball, the other grasping
halfway up the slim obelisk.

"The Trylon and Perisphere,"
my mother smiles, taking it
into her own remembered hands
for a moment, as if
that explained everything.

**

The Valley of Ashes

between Manhattan and West Egg
in *The Great Gatsby*—that beckoning
landfill Robert Moses told Grover Whalen
to go bulldoze
into tomorrow.

The greatest civil engineering feat
of the century, the newsreels proclaimed.
Twelve hundred and sixteen acres, transformed
into a one hundred and fifty-five million dollar
wonderland, as if by magic.

The Trylon and Perisphere centered
the converging grid of pastel
avenues, color-coded, presided over by a giant
George Washington.

When did I learn those two buildings
were white, pure white, the only pure white
permitted on those acres? For years

I imagined them the discolor
of ashes, the ashes before,
the ashes that followed, 1939.

**

They

both turned 26 that year, both living
in New York, free
and unmet. Yet they must have gone

44

to Flushing Meadows, separately unpocketed
their seventy-five cents—two of the millions
rung up on the seven-story National
Cash Register—to see the same signs
and wonders. I wonder which one

bought the souvenir ashtray, bright
as a Depression penny, and which one
brought it through the years, saved it
for my unborn eyes.

**

Futurama

The most popular exhibit, where General Motors
predicted and manufactured, in equal measure.
You'd take your seat and zeppelin
above a new America of superhighways,
cars compelled by radio to absolute
safety, bonsai growing around brimming lakes
with real water—a model
that convinced you it wasn't
a model, it was what
America would and should become—the final
miniature street you saw
becoming the real street, full-sized,
you walked out into, I HAVE SEEN
THE FUTURE buttoned
to your shirt, your dress.

And they had.

**

Democracity

What is the point of showing such houses . . . when . . .
no one in the world has the money to buy them?
          —E. L. Doctorow, *World's Fair*

Inside the Perisphere, a vision
with subdivisions—Edens
enbubbled, which you circumnavigated
to see from every
angle, from your moving
sidewalk, a world that didn't
move, that remained
perfect—homes so much
like the one my parents would buy
nineteen years later, the mortgage
paid off six months before
my mother died, one year after I'd bought
my own mortgage
in Travelers Rest, South Carolina.

**

The Westinghouse Pavilion

had its own movie, starring
the four Middletons—mother, father,
Babs, and Bud—come from the Midwest
for summer vacation. Now, on my own
TV/VCR, I see them approaching
not Flushing Meadows, but
a sleepy Long Island hamlet, Huntington—

their grandma's house—just minutes east
of my wife's childhood,
minutes west of Walt Whitman's, a half-hour
north of my own.

All our subdivisions erased by the recorded
past, in color worthy
of *Gone with the Wind.*

Off to The Fair, where it's all
Westinghouse: Elektro, the world's first
talking robot (*OK, Toots!*);
Mrs. Modern's dishwasher
soundly defeating Mrs. Drudge's frenetic
sink and rag; Picture Radio,
where Bud mugs for his father watching
not him but the tiny monitor
across the room.

For the finale, Babs and her new
Westinghouse boyfriend, hand in hand, watch
the fireworks coming out
of the water, firing into
the night—while he promises, in the middle
of the August explosions, they haven't
seen anything yet.

**

The Entertainment Zone: 1940

It had become pretty obvious what tomorrow was going
to be like, and the day after tomorrow was far away.
                                        —Jason Robards

That second summer,
when you were sick of the sanitized
future, the aerated bread, Asbestos—
The Magic Mineral, the cows
on the Borden Rotolactor, The Torch
of Eternal Friendship
at the Japanese Pavilion, here's what
you went for: LifeSaver's parachute
jump, the jitterbug contests,
Salvador Dali's *Dream of Venus*
(chic underwater cheesecake), and Elektro's
unauthorized wife—who never spoke but whose hips
circled, clockwise, counter-
clockwise, when you pressed the button
of either nipple.

And the Odditorium, which my mother
would have tearfully loved: the man
with webbed feet, the limbless woman
in a basket, and Albert the Giant
who'd remove his rings for a dollar, to slip
over her wrists.

And my father? Would he have slipped
out, stayed away, glimpsed it all
from a distance? Or, emboldened
by a few beers, would he have gaped along
with the rest?

48

**

The Next Fair

A quarter century later
we didn't go. The Perisphere
long gone, gobbled by a wiffleball
with bare, burnished continents, and oceans
of empty space. My mother—

who'd driven coal trucks at fourteen
to Philadelphia, who'd worked
as secretary, sales clerk, nurse's
aide, real-estate agent, school bus
driver, mechanic—was housekeeping

for Robert Moses! She swore
the old man would hand her
free tickets for the family, must have
muttered hints while she emptied
the ashtrays, vacuumed around his feet.

By the end of the summer, she'd
quit, muttering about the small hearts
of the rich. Or maybe
she'd just seen too much
of the future, already.

**

2006

What does it mean, this twentieth century
from which I've emerged
alive? I hung around
for half of it, minus twelve
seconds or so: born in one small Asian
war, twelve years after the Soviet Pavilion
rose from the garbage of Queens and Kings.

Now, the Age of America: global
warming, the Hydra apocalypse of hurricanes
and four-dollar gasoline, General Motors
choking on highways filled
with Japanese cars.

Lithuania, which disappeared before its own
exhibit, is now a nation
once more. Vanished
Czechoslovakia is two.

But no dirigibles dock
at floating, rotating terminals; no helicopters roost
on our separate roofs. Our streets are still black
and white, Democracities,
gated communities.
Floor to ceiling, we're still
removing "the magic mineral."

Towers have fallen
like Poland and France.

And yet they survived, my mother and father,
for a while, a long while, really—
to meet in his hospital room
after the war, and marry, and move
a bit farther south

as I would move farther south still.
Is Florida my future? I hope not.
Last month, Barbara and I paid off our mortgage
at fifty-five. Free and clear
till our cat disappeared,

the cat we'd had for nine years, who'd walked straight
from the pine thicket, eyed my lawn chair, and jumped
into my lap. Question asked

and answered, only
by a summer's day.

A day walks into our lives, from whatever
forest, into the sun, and then
walks back. I never saw
my parents die, either.

And every one of us will disappear
from some other, some other day—
if we're lucky, to be remembered
for that moment when we
were tomorrow. As we asked
or answered that first question. As we made
that future we never saw coming.

**

V. But to Begin It

The Clarinet

Three bucks a month, to rent the clarinet
I hadn't played in years, my mother said.
Flat on my back, in bed, I held the magazine
at arm's length toward the ceiling. "I'm retired."

She'd just picked up the mail for Saturday,
the latest invoice from the music store.
Would it upset me if she brought it back?
"Why should I care?"

                            She closed the door, spoke through it.
"Take anything that's yours out of the case."

The case held nothing but the instrument.
I freed it from its velvet, sliding the ebony
over the cork connections, moistened the reed—
a taste I had forgotten. Like a Popsicle
long after all the ice was licked away.

When I'd been in the sixth grade, getting bored
with band, I learned to read by ear—mocking
the parts of other instruments, switching
from saxophone, to trumpet, to trombone.
One day the band director, very careful
not to look at me, explained his first
principle of music: *It's far better to play
the wrong note at precisely the right time
than the right note too early or too late.*
Of course, he'd rather have two rights together.

I didn't take the hint, accompanying
every soloist at every concert.

My room contained a bed, a dresser/bookcase
and a turntable/radio. No chairs.
So I strolled along the carpet colored sea
and played the only song a clarinet
had taken all the way to Number One.

I'd memorized
each note four years ago
and every time Mom laughed
"Is that the radio?"

"Stranger on the Shore," by Acker Bilk.
By the end, though, I was crying, softly,
for what or whom I couldn't figure out.
I'd never been particularly fond
of playing. Maybe those tears were for the last
possibility of my own music
filling that room, making its own chair.

Whatever I thought, it didn't last for long.
Dismembering the instrument, dry-eyed,
I went back to the bed I'd made, and read.

So ends my story. But another one
must have happened, on the other side
of those thin walls, within the dining room
or kitchen. My mother's seated, listening
to music she's all too familiar with,
my laid-off father with his newspaper
across the table—both knowing three bucks
could buy two weeks of junior high school lunches,
half a tank of gas, a Sunday dinner.
Those thoughts would feed her Monday morning, when
I'd left for school, and she unlatched my door.

Uncles

December 1978

The day before Mom's funeral, like bats,
they fluttered in at sunset—Joseph, Tom,
Steve, Oscar, Henry, Eddie, John, and Bart.
Hungover and determined, they'd all come

from central Pennsylvania, in two cars.
They trudged into my father's house—little
men, stooped from mining anthracite, eight dwarfs
in search of their first ending, single file.

So long they'd told the story of eleven
brothers and sisters. My father served them shots
and beers past midnight—when, praise be to Heaven,
they all staggered out. Their unlit cigarettes,

their wrinkled faces broken umbrellas
stained with rain, for their lost Cinderella.

This Branching Room

This branching room is open to the weather.
No roof, just rafters. Walls invisible
as windows. Trees, shrubbery a picture
of what, after some rain, I'll call my world.
I hope newspaper mulch will save the flowers.
The sod I tread on's just too dry to grow.

I green upon the memories that grow
illegible as newsprint in the weather.
I can't recall the first time I brought flowers
(Roses? Lilies?) to the now-invisible
bedmates who brought my body into this world,
and turned my empty frame into a picture.

I wish—oh, how I wish—I could still picture
my mother and my father. But they grow
ever more distant, inhabiting the world
of photographs—that unchanging weather
where living faces flatten, invisible
even to the touch, like last year's flowers.

My parents filled their yard with living flowers.
That's something even now I can still picture,
summoning out of time and space, in visible
form, zinnias and marigolds—that grow
regardless of my Carolina weather
and the indifferent earth that soils the world.

I stand in what I've come to call my world:
three acres of well-orchestrated flowers,
understory plants tuned to the weather
of Appalachian forest I can picture
even when I close my eyes to grow
silent, shadows stretching to night, invisible.

So much around me is invisible.
My mother's ashes, scattered in my world,
before my father told me where. I grow
less certain, as the decades pass, what flowers
he spread them under. I can't even picture
his urn in my own hand, and the weather

that invisible summer day. White flowers
whirled underneath the season's moving picture.
I grow toward the end of my own weather.

Reckoning

Those Hoogendorn hollies
hunch blotchy, half-dead
under loblollies—
whose needles unthread

every December
to litter the lawn
we raked in November.
(It was overrun

by ghosts of crabapples,
red and white oaks.
Two Japanese maples
abandoned their cloaks.)

So beautifully bare
for almost a week!
Grass, branches, air
beyond all critique.

But now yellow pine straw
and berryless blight.
The first we foresaw.
The second? Not quite.

But to Begin It

Somehow we've bumbled into
The Blind Garden—
a square ring
strung with braille
among leaves of mints,
marjoram and rosemary, ready
to be seen by the tag team
of fingers and nose

but that our four eyes gratefully
identify, taking we think it all
in—till we round the far corner and find
next to the exit, a fountain
with brass cymbals playing water
music we never heard, meant
not just to end the piece
but to begin it.

VI. The First Days

The First Days

for Cecilia Czettl Szigeti (1919-2002)
and William Szigeti (1920-2005)

1.

Before breakfast, the two of us
in her kitchen, sitting
in silence—she liked silence
too—I would boil the water, steep
our tea in the old pot (from England?)

and we'd drink, cup after cup,

till her husband staggered, half-asleep
from shift work at Pan Am, into
her morning, demanding coffee.

She'd huff
to the stove, empty the kettle
into his chipped, favorite mug
primed with instant, and mutter
Not even clean sheets. I cross the ocean
for you, and not even clean sheets.

She'd wait till he left
for his favorite chair, then smile for me,
her son-in-law, across that vanishing table
as if nothing had happened, as I remember

it all now, twenty or thirty
or forty years later, drinking
that same Lipton tea, alone

**

2.

Perhaps they *were* clean, just
not ironed, when she came to New York
in 1947, fresh from eight years
in England.

She'd left Hungary
at nineteen, full of her own life—
a farmer's last daughter, half-spoiled
by half-sisters nearly old enough to be
her mother, lost giving birth
to the next child. They'd seen her

three years old, forced by uncles, by aunts
to kiss the swollen corpse goodbye.
They'd taken pity, saved her
from the worst chores, let her play
with the cats, feed the chickens.

For years she longed after her mother's
earrings, stealing into her father's room
just to stare—finally piercing herself
with a sewing needle, so she could wear them
till she healed.

But in 1939, she left them behind.
(Her one full sister, Julia, wore those gold circles
till a Russian soldier mercifully
ripped them out of her ears
without touching her.)

At Seven Oaks, in that spring
and summer before the war, Cecilia
cooked for the servants
who served her, cleaning
her room, washing, ironing
her sheets. From her own window

she'd watch garden parties on grass
tennis courts, thinking about
that life, her life, her dowry
growing day by day.

I thought I was in heaven.

**

3.

The bricks that never disappeared.

His grandfather brought him down
the hill, to the abandoned factory, to carry his punishment
from one end to the other, day after day.

Born in Serbia, swaddled in Brooklyn, sent back
to the family that disowned his mother
for marrying a peasant. Sent back

because 1933 was softer in Serbia
than in Brooklyn. Sent back with his
baby sister, to take care of her.

He slept in the barn.
She slept in the house.
What happened there

God knows. But they trusted no one
like each other, their whole lives
another seventy years.

On Saint Nicholas Day, her shoes brimmed
with garlic, his with clinkers
four Decembers. Sent back

finally, in steerage, old enough
to work in America, old enough
to find his father gone, dead,

his mother living with a new man,
a diamond cutter, with his own two-story house
on Gates Avenue.

**

4.

But on that first day, summer
1972, when I brought home his daughter
after our first date, tennis,
and he invited me to stay
for pan-fried chicken on the patio

his wife seemed
happy—not at all
put out by his impulsive
hospitality. Or perhaps she'd seen
my white shirt and shorts

on that green Caledonia
lawn, from between her clean
lace curtains, and suggested
it herself.

**

5.

Mary, the Austrian, had ruled
the Seven Oaks kitchen *auf Deutsch*.
Interned in September, she gave
her *liebchen* a farewell book, *So kocht man in Wien!*
How One Cooks in Vienna!

Olive green cover, Gothic script
soon thumbed to tatters
while she battered and buttered,
boiled and fried, for both servants
and masters.

Until her own dubious tongue
and passport forced her
to London, inside an ever-
narrowing red circle, to work
cooking bombs

British bombs
that her future American husband would drop
on her own *Unterradling,* her own family!
Or so she swore to her American television
above her American sink.

She hated war.
Yet she whispered to me of those London
nights, those deafening tunnels, bombs everywhere
above her, crocheting now, 1941
the happiest time of her life.

**

6.

North Atlantic, 1944, bound
for England, the B-17 imperceptibly
sinking, wings heavy with ice, visibility

down to nothing.
Staff Sergeant Szigeti, Top Turret Gunner
and Flight Engineer, made the captain

backfire the engines—shaking
an aluminum hummingbird, fresh
from a cold bath—now free

but still going down, the gray waves
close enough to lap the landing gear
had it been lowered

till the engines restarted, and the plane
slowly rose, humming toward the future.

**

7.

So many stories,
so many *things*.

1945, returning from a mission
he had no right to return from
he joyfully bought a lavaliere, peridots green
as meadow grass, damn
the expense *(probably
pawned by a princess!)*
just to see her wear it.

Both on bicycles, in the countryside, caught
in a sudden shower, taking shelter
under the English oak, taking time
to examine the teapot they'd just won
at a church raffle.

*

1947, brought to Brooklyn, married
in a false church, with a diamond ring she wouldn't
wear, cleaning, sewing for his family
in a house with no doors
his stepfather couldn't open.

1949, a new mother, yet eager
to welcome her own father
to America, shepherd him to Pittsburgh, to live
with her half-sister—till she learned
he strayed off the plane at La Guardia
into the unfenced water, and the police
blamed her for the bloated corpse.

*

1952, his wife diagnosed with TB, Barb
and Billy in the car, crying, at the gas station,
when his TV repairman at the next pump asks
How ya doin and he tells him, weeping,
and the man and his wife take the kids for a year
and become Uncle Gabby and Auntie Ann,
her lilacs still in our yard.

*

Cured, back home, in Caledonia now
listening to his mother call her
a thief, when the old woman comes over
for Sunday dinner, sneaks off to hide
her diamonds, and promptly
forgets where.

While she labored for decades, cleaning
her neighbors' kitchens, washing
and ironing, to buy U.S. Savings Bonds
for her children, stashing them where
they'd never be found
and almost weren't.

*

When he learned his father wasn't dead
but in Creedmore State Hospital
and when he drove up, heard
the first orderly say he'd have to pay
for twenty years' care
and left, not giving his name.

To pay, forty years later
for a tombstone to place
on his father's numbered grave.

To take his wife to Sunday dinner
at his baby sister's, where she'd refused to go
for half a century, to see Cecilia's Alzheimer's
smile, before and beyond
forgiveness, outshining even her proudly
spread fingers, her first wedding ring.

To die himself, three years later, and leave
a two car garage with room
for no cars, a helicopter
in pieces, a house heaped with gleanings
of rummage sales, impassable hallways
and a basement burgeoning with swollen
cans, swaddled in mildew, all
on an acre lot in Caledonia
worth a million dollars.

His last words: *Let it be.*

**

8.

In 1945, they'd both seen
the sneak preview
at his base—*I Live in Grosvenor Square.*

March 1997, the day after
her cancer operation, he looks at her—
really looks. *It almost depicted our lives.*

Watching the tape, I'm surprised
he uses that word
depicted.

He'd taken the American hero, Dean Jagger,
on real combat missions. *The guy
didn't have to do that.*

They could've just flown around Yeldon Field.
They might've been killed
just like in the movie.

**

9.

The very end of another tape, this one
filmed two days before:

I lived between the Underground
and the bus stop. If you missed one
you got the other. I worked
in a factory there.
I went to three movies
a day, on my day off.

"Now you're in the movies."

She doesn't smile.
She's already told her daughter
every war, they take a piece away, and tomorrow
they'll turn her inside out.

I was living on Abbey Road
when I met your father. I was over two years
in that Greek restaurant. Part time.
I was never lonesome.
I got plenty of tips. America
is another story. I wasn't exactly crazy
about it when—

**

VII. Dead Man's Curve

A Wedding Wish

We look. Do they? If blindness were a lens
it would be blank as the side windows of
a stretch limo—our noses pressed against
our own reflections. Here, since God is love,

behold the man! And wife! Smile for their camera!
We once were the celebrities inside.
Perhaps the chauffeur's just a chimera
and nobody's been taken for a ride,

not yet. This summer, weddings every week
it seems. Gifting their kids, we keep the faith
with friends and colleagues. We've become the meek
who can't inherit but bequeath the earth.

The singer and the pianist began
three times today, before they got it right,
inside the church. An uncle's violin
howled like four strung-out calicos in heat.

All amateurs! What else can old farts say
at times like these? Especially in words.
Better to wave the couple on their way
and blow soap bubbles for them. Rice kills birds.
Funny we never thought of such a thing.
Their car begins to move. Dead reckoning.

Two Become One Flesh

with apologies to Mark 10:8

He can't hoist either hand above his head.
Her feet won't stand more than a dozen steps.
He's too nearsighted for the DMV.
Her fingers feel like she's got mittens on.
When did his legs get too long for his arms?
When did her arms get too short for her eyes?
He can't smell newsprint pressed against his nose.
She can't hear *Thanks* while helping with his socks.

The kitchen bulb burns out for both and each.

She drives the car. He strides into Best Buy.
Back home, he brings the stool. She stretches high.
He shouts the recipe. She bakes the quiche.
He listens for the *ding*. She finds the plates.
He cuts. They eat. She tells him how it tastes.

Blueberries

All June
and July, berries,
enough berries, more
than enough, berries for the birds
and us! Each morning
we'd go out in the still
and savor, marveling
in low sunlight at their burgeoning
abacus, subtracting
the ripest, the best.

Now Carolina August
and only a few
remain—ones we'd have passed
over, or thrown away, it only seems
moments before. Yet we pluck,
and find, in their barely
bitter, a remembered
flavor—then happen upon one
cluster our soured mouths swear
the sweetest of the season.

Dead Man's Curve

for Jan Berry (1941-2004)

Well the last thing I remember Doc
I started to swerve—it's one of the great
howlers in Stone Age Rock
right up there with Teen Angel's
unauthorized ring retrieval
that fateful night the car was stalled
upon the railroad tracks
and The Leader of the Pack's laying down
the longest strip of rubber
in the history of vinyl.

No no no no nonononono!

Those brief, twisted moments
when our sputtering lives, cluttered with homework
and hormones and hectoring, seemed turntabled
by genuine tragedy, death abetted
by automobile—pulling us out
of freshman biology
unfathomable as fuel injection.

And now we're still here, trying our best
not to catch up—replacing knees,
hips, shoulders, as if
we're our own custom cars
ready to Viagra into infinity.

We ease them into Stingrays,
XKEs, Mustangs, Priuses, whatever
but they're really just the oldest
form of mass transit—
taking us back to school, no brakes
on this baby, sliding into the curve
that is, simply, the earth's.

Symbolic Gestures

I went down to the demonstration
To get my fair share of abuse.
　　　　　　　—The Rolling Stones

That fall, the guy
who looked like Harry Belafonte
got a white puppy
from the Humane Society

so he could fix
it himself. Even though pets
couldn't stay in the dorm, we
didn't rat him out.

We knew it was just
a symbolic gesture.
When it kept shitting
in the hallways, and some

anal retentives we never could
positively identify scooped up
a whole week's worth to dump
onto his threshold, he threw

the dog out the window, shouting
"Leave it alone!"
He lived on the fourth floor.
The dog died

eventually. Now
the question became how
to avoid the rotting corpse
of racism. "I'll sleep

with him," Amy said, "let him
knock me around
a little, at least until
he lets me bury the dog."

What can I say?
In 1969 it passed
for a good idea.
Wherever you looked

people threw bodies
around like confetti
and every day, if
you were lucky, you

picked yourself up
for the next parade.

VIII. Forty Years North of Dreamland

Forty Years North of Dreamland

Here, being visible is being white . . .
     —"The Auroras of Autumn"

1.

Too far away, too late, I never saw
Dreamland. It rhymed with Margaret Mitchell's wind,
now just as gone. The swimming lake's swamp-forest,
the nine-hole golf course razed for home improvement—
Lowe's, standing where Depression mill boys gathered
to carry woods and irons of the rich,
to make more money on good Saturdays
than any linthead father earned all week.

I live about a seven-minute drive
due north of where the kids from Monaghan,
Dunean, Poe, Brandon, Union Bleachery
walked every summer with their sweaty nickels
to cool off in the dream of T. F. Floyd.
His house survives, an upscale restaurant.

**

2.

His house survives, an upscale restaurant
where some of those same children, now retired,
sit comfortably among us newcomers
and spend more on the Special of the Day
than three months' rent on vanished birthplaces.
At dusk, we watch them looking through the glass
that lamplight turns half mirror—distant faces,
willows lost not just among the sight
of phantom water, but its sound, below—

until Glenn Miller's *Moonlight Serenade*
drifts from the ceiling's speakers, followed by
the Jimmy Dorsey Orchestra's *Green Eyes*,
the sweetest song of 1941,
the one the lifeguard played, over and over.

**

3.

The song the lifeguard played, over and over,
after his shift. He'd open Dreamland Lake
at 10 AM, clear snakes and snapping turtles
from the sand, watch new wives and new babies.
At lunch, the ones who knew Mama from church
would bring him half a sandwich, or a peach,
before they had to leave for home and husbands.
Before he had to chase the fifth-grade boys
from knotholes in the boards along the back side
of the changing rooms. Then all the girls
from Parker High would puddle at his feet,
begging him to trip the pavilion jukebox
for them that night—when they'd sneak back to dance,
after Dreamland had closed, officially.

**

4.

Before Dreamland had closed, officially,
a preacher would drive down New Buncombe Road
most Sunday afternoons. He'd set up loudspeakers
in front of the pavilion or the clubhouse
and holler, "Don't go down to that hell hole!"

Throughout the thirties, every year, big bands
headed to Atlanta, Asheville, Charlotte
would stop here at the foot of Paris Mountain
to play for thousands. But after the second war
the private swimming pools and television
accomplished what evangelism couldn't.
One night, the empty old pavilion burned.

A couple of wars later, in the ruins,
a Vietnam vet builds a bamboo hut.

**

5.

A Vietnam vet built a bamboo hut
somewhere down below the old golf course.
His name was Harold. He'd come out at night,
climb up the hill to Floyd's converted house
to trade some junk—bent signs, illegible
with rust, abandoned putters, ancient Coke
and Pepsi bottles rescued from the mud—
for a few Miller Ponies at the bar.
I learn about him from the owner's son,
who tried to shield him from the customers—
all white tonight, a mere coincidence,
for every color's green is welcome here
and has been since the 1970s,
back when my wife and I first moved to Greenville.

**

6.

Back when my wife and I first moved to Greenville,
nobody spoke of Dreamland. But we saw
an old gas station, same side of the road,
with broken pipes beside the service bays
still labeled WHITE and COLORED. At the college
where I'd soon teach, I joined the tennis club.
One evening, after a long match, I watched
the woman trusted with the restroom key
smile softly to a black kid on his bike.
"That door's locked. Try the other one, in back."

There was no other door—just screens of bushes
we'd use when the attendant wasn't there.
She was a local, born and born again.
She might've gone to Dreamland as a girl.

**

7.

She might've gone to Dreamland as a girl.
But by the start of FDR's third term
she would've been too old to while away
her weekdays there. She might've worked downtown
in Penney's, or in Eckerd's Cut Rate Drugs.
She would've taken the Duke Power Trolley
to the last stop—North Franklin/Blue Ridge Drive—
right after work, and walked a country mile
before she changed into her bathing suit
or just slipped on her jitterbugging shoes.

Or maybe she found work at Dreamland Lake—
at the concession stand, the dressing room.
She never would have chased Coloreds away.
They would've known, not bothered to have come.

**

8.

They should've known, not bothered to have come.
But they were picking blackberries nearby
when Mr. T. F. Floyd saw them. They could
have been his grandchildren, but for the grace
of Jesus God. He'd built this very house
with old Black Remmy, after the Great War.
The two of them cleared stones from the golf course
and made a jigsaw puzzle fit to live in.

What did the world expect farm boys to do?
Walk all the way downtown, sneak into movies?
He whistled from his elevated porch,
told them to get their sorry backsides in
the water. Today was hot, goddammit! "Boys,
in this town, Hell stays in the cotton mills!"

**

9.

In this town, Hell stayed inside cotton mills
where air conditioning was nothing but
a "feasibility initiative"

discussed by bureaucrats in Washington
determined to increase defense production.
They funded mobile X-ray clinics—TB
screening all along the Textile Crescent,
testing weavers during cigarette
and coffee breaks, to cull the cutting floor.

Three shifts, plenty of work for everyone.
The only time production ever stopped
was when some fool got caught between the rollers.
That, or the blackout drill in '42,
when the whole city turned invisible.

**

10.

When the whole city turned invisible,
the German subs off the Atlantic coast
were sinking silhouetted cargo ships
faster than America could build them.
New bicycles could only be obtained
"for wartime purposes." The army raised
its volunteer enlistment age to fifty.
Belk-Simpson ran an illustrated ad—
It's patriotic to be beautiful!
And from the month-old Greenville Army Air Base
Captain Hoffman's B-24 bomber
flew all the way past Dreamland. The next day
he analyzed the blackout for the press.
"This one's the most effective I have seen."

**

11.

This one's the most effective I have seen—
period instruments and costuming,
mustached, brass-buttoned, polished volunteers
conducted by a musicologist.
The climate-controlled auditorium's
packed for the Textile Heritage Band concert.

Their audience is equally authentic.
This afternoon, dark hair's almost as rare
as dark faces. Only a few dyed women.
Every man is gray, or bald, or both.

The youngster on euphonium's the star,
gets a belated, slow-mo standing O.
I wonder if the geriatrics here
worked at the mills, and walked to Dreamland Lake.

**

12.

Work at the mill, and walk to Dreamland Lake—
where you could sit beneath the willow trees
and let the distant thunderstorm of looms
evaporate. Your ears clear once again,
you climb the high dive, try the Spinning Top,
take your turn at the outdoor bowling alley,
a few more turns around the roller rink.
Rub some Noxzema on your sunburned shoulders,
then hear the latest music from the jukebox.

You watch old men who hadn't been your age
since the last century—now lawyers, doctors—
playing bad golf until the sun's all gone.

A kid carries their bags to their new cars.
You'll never be like them, you tell yourself.

**

13.

You'd never be like them, you told yourself,
and yet you are. Like every one of them.
You've matched the doctors, lawyers, by degrees.
Your cars are new. You walk for exercise.
Each summer, you spend hours in the garden
with work that drove the farmers to the mills.
Your house, on the same side of Paris Mountain
as T. F. Floyd's, now overlooks a park
where kids who don't belong to country clubs
can skateboard, rollerblade, scream down the slides,
soar on the swing sets, sneak down by the creek
under the sweetgum trees. You see it from
your elevated foyer, hear it from your deck.
You close your eyes. The decades disappear.

**

14.

You close your eyes, the decades disappear.
When I was seven, 1958,
I woke one summer morning to the news:
Our family would move to California!

We sold our home in Hempstead just before
my dad's new job fell through. We had two weeks
to find a place we could afford, move in.

A little spec house near abandoned farms
long gone to scrub and weeds, miles farther east
out on Long Island. In a new suburb
destined to be white. But down the street

Deer Lake—a place to fish, and swim, and dream.
It closed after I went away to college.
Too far away, too late, I never saw.

**

IX. My Mother Teaches Me to Type

Sixty Winters

What youthful mother, a shape upon her lap . . .
Would think her son, did she but see that shape
With sixty or more winters on its head,
A compensation for the pang of his birth,
Or the uncertainty of his setting forth?
                    —W. B. Yeats, b. June 13, 1865

I

We've thrown a party every New Year's Eve,
my wife and I, since 1981.
But she'd say 1980. I believe
we start at "Happy Birthday" (mine)—not when
the first carloads of guests trudge up the drive.
Is it *it* when it ends? When it begins?
Since I came out twelve seconds after twelve
forgive my being ontological.

II

You'd think I'd have another year to go
since I'll be turning only fifty-nine
this 20-10. Unfortunately, no.
The cork pangs from the Extra Brut champagne.
Like Yeats, I set forth at the age of zero.
Unlike his vision, Capricorn's my sign.
So sixty winters now are on my head
although my snow is pretty thinly spread.

III

My mother died December first—still fall,
two years and change before I turned thirty.
So this is Minus Thirty-Two, by all
accounts, for her—Plus Thirty-Two for me.
We both were too goddamn mathematical
I hear her say, *or you'd have been tax-free.*
One lost deduction. For a busted nation
I guess that's bordering on compensation.

IV

Dead more than half my age. Now nearly hers,
I think she'd be amused, though, not displeased,
beholding my persistence. Not that there's
much to the winters here—maybe a freeze
three nights a week, frost on the junipers.
A few days even brush the seventies.
Once you get moving, you feel almost young
most dawns, Marie. Birds sing your mother tongue.

Bees in Lavender

Only man's sick of blood,
and man's not so sick of it either.
                    —Robert Frost

Workaholics, hijackers
hover, bending every stalk
over in this city of stalks, un-
burdening each small window of nectar.

Only they can see through
to honey.

In a world for the moment
without birds, without breezes, without butterflies
they fill the mind
like the evening news
after a bad day.

Near the south end
of the newly mulched garden, their dance
turns to random music—something
between a radio reduced to static
and a dying electric razor.
I try to follow just

one—who fills its one
note with seventeen flowers
before I lose sight of it in the swarm
of likenesses. Lavender sways

toward sunset, becoming
the mirror that won't break, the windows
that keep falling.
On this feedback loop
in dying color, bees

become planes, become bodies
become planes, become bodies
until they all vanish at once.

Steady as vengeance,
flowers arise,
blue matches here and now
and now.

My Mother Teaches Me to Type

Now is the time for all good men
to come to the aid of their country.
Letters, words, open spaces
her hands learned by heart
in 1942, for her audition in the towers
of New York. Twenty years later

I'm only eleven, but still
she's no man, either. Twenty fingers, suspended
over the stiff keys. We take turns
closing our eyes, filling
blank paper as if the world
depended upon our play.

On any keyboard, that sentence
still draws the deepest
music from my hands. Eyes shut
or open, light, no light
no matter. *Now is the time . . .*
For her sake, come home.

In the Natural History Museum

for Caroline Tevis-Bernardy

Don't touch the world the guard says (to the child
stretching toward the great, inviting globe)
as if the Prime Meridian's defiled.
A tiny fingertip's an Anglophobe

in an obedient instant. And the pink
of England is preserved from anarchy
once more—by our commanding, kindred link
to Reading Gaol, in Washington, DC.

You weren't there, but someday this story might reach
your eyes or ears. Then thank your lucky stars,
your hands, grasping the sand of Folly Beach,
the red clay of Berea—wherever you were,

and are, and will be, as you press upon
this crumbling earth, as gently as you can.

Good Luck

You've seen the flicks
with the blasted hero, hunkering
in the foxhole
bleeding into black
and white, clenched teeth promising
the camera at least he'll take one
of them with him.

All of us
mangled, by birth, labor,
marriage, vowing
to lead somebody else
into the ground.

Lord, when I'm about
to go under, let me
swear instead
to leave one behind.

About the Author

Gilbert Allen writes poems and short fiction. His books include *In Everything, Second Chances, Commandments at Eleven, Driving to Distraction, Catma,* and *The Final Days of Great American Shopping.* A longtime resident of upstate South Carolina, he was elected to The South Carolina Academy of Authors, the state's literary hall of fame, in 2014. He is the Bennette E. Geer Professor of Literature Emeritus at Furman University.

CPSIA information can be obtained
at www.ICGtesting.com
Printed in the USA
LVHW081351271120
672843LV00005B/16